# Billboard

MW00558981

## #1 HITS OF THE 1970s • A SHEET MUSIC COMPENDIUM

Produced by
Alfred Music Publishing Co., Inc.
P.O. Box 10003
Van Nuys, CA 91410-0003
alfred.com

Printed in USA.

ISBN-10: 0-7390-6969-1
ISBN-13: 978-0-7390-6969-1

# Contents

| SONG | ARTIST | PAGE |
|------|--------|------|

# 50 WAYS TO LEAVE YOUR LOVER

Words and Music by
PAUL SIMON

6

# AFTERNOON DELIGHT

Words and Music by
BILL DANOFF

In a moderately slow country 2 ♩ = 76

*Verse 1:*

find my ba - by, gon - na hold her tight, gon - na grab some af - ter - noon_____ de - light._____ My

mot - to's al - ways been "When it's right, it's right." Why wait un - til the mid - dle of a cold dark night

Afternoon Delight - 7 - 1

*Verse 2:*

out this morn - ing feel - ing so po - lite, I al - ways thought a fish could not be caught who

did - n't bite.__ But you got some bait a - wait - ing and I think I might like nib - bl - ing a lit - tle af - ter -

*D.S. ℅ al Coda*

*Coda*

noon de - light.__

af - ter - noon__ de - light.__

*Guitar solo:*

# ANGIE

Words and Music by
MICK JAGGER and
KEITH RICHARDS

Slowly ♩ = 66

Angie - 7 - 1

Angie - 7 - 5

# AMERICAN PIE

Words and Music by
DON McLEAN

**D.S. al Coda**

day the mu - sic died.    And they were sing - in'.

**CODA**

This - 'll be the day __ that I ____ die. ____

*Additional Lyrics*

2. Now for ten years we've been on our own,
And moss grows fat on a rollin' stone
But that's not how it used to be
When the jester sang for the king and queen
In a coat he borrowed from James Dean
And a voice that came from you and me
Oh and while the king was looking down,
The jester stole his thorny crown
The courtroom was adjourned,
No verdict was returned
And while Lenin read a book on Marx
The quartet practiced in the park
And we sang dirges in the dark
The day the music died
We were singin'... bye-bye... etc.

3. Helter-skelter in the summer swelter
The birds flew off with a fallout shelter
Eight miles high and fallin' fast,
it landed foul on the grass
The players tried for a forward pass,
With the jester on the sidelines in a cast
Now the half-time air was sweet perfume
While the sergeants played a marching tune
We all got up to dance
But we never got the chance
'Cause the players tried to take the field,
The marching band refused to yield
Do you recall what was revealed
The day the music died
We started singin'... bye-bye... etc.

4. And there we were all in one place,
A generation lost in space
With no time left to start again
So come on, Jack be nimble, Jack be quick,
Jack Flash sat on a candlestick
'Cause fire is the devil's only friend
And as I watched him on the stage
My hands were clenched in fists of rage
No angel born in hell
Could break that Satan's spell
And as the flames climbed high into the night
To light the sacrificial rite
I saw Satan laughing with delight
The day the music died
He was singin'... bye-bye... etc.

# BABE

Words and Music by
DENNIS DeYOUNG

near.

My train is go - ing;___ I see it in___ your eyes,___

the love, the need, your tears.

But I'll be lone - ly with-out_

_____ you,

and I'll need your love to see me through.

So, please be - lieve me;___ my heart is in___ your hands,_

and I'll be miss - ing

you.

'Cause you know it's you,___ babe,___ when-

ev - er I___ get wea - ry and I've had e - nough,_ feel like giv - ing up._ You know it's

you,___ babe,_ giv - ing me___ the cour - age and the strength I need._

Please be - lieve___ that it's true. Babe, I love you._

*To Coda* ⊕ *Bridge:*

*D.S.* 𝄋 *al Coda*

You know it's

36

*Coda*
*Verse 2:*

2. Babe, I'm leav - ing;____ I'll say it once__ a - gain,__

and some-how try_____ to smile. I know the feel - ing____ we're

try - ing to for - get, if on - ly for a - while.

'Cause I'll be lone - ly with-out_____ you, and I'll need your love to see me

Babe - 6 - 5

through.

But please be - lieve me;___ my heart is in___ your hands,__ 'cause

**Slightly slower**

I'll be miss - ing you.

Babe, I love you.__

Babe, I love you.___

Oo,_____ babe.

# BENNIE AND THE JETS

Words and Music by
ELTON JOHN and
BERNIE TAUPIN

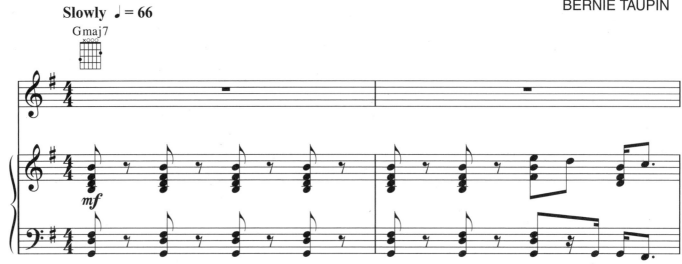

Bennie and the Jets - 4 - 1

light's hit - ting some - thing that's been known to change the weath - er.
be they're___ blind - ed,_____ but Ben - nie makes them age - less.

We'll kill the fat - ted calf___ to - night, so___ stick a - round._____ You're
We shall___ sur - vive;_ let us take our - selves a - long._____ Where we

gon - na hear e - lec - tric mu - sic, sol - id walls of sound.___ Say,
fight our par - ents out in the streets_ to find who's right and who's wrong._____
*...end solo)*

*Chorus:*

Can - dy and Ron - nie, have you seen them yet?_ Oh,_____ but they're so___ spaced out.___ B - B - B - B - B

# BLACK WATER

Words and Music by
PATRICK SIMMONS

Black Water - 6 - 1

And I ain't got no wor - ries 'cause I

ain't in no hur - ry __ at all.

Well, if it rains, I don't care, __ don't make no

# BABY COME BACK

Words and Music by
JOHN CROWLEY
and PETER BECKETT

1. Spend-in'

Baby Come Back - 5 - 1

Noth-in' left for me,    ain't there    noth-in' left for me?_____    Ba-by, come back,

___ you.    I was    wrong_ and I just___can't live.

# BLINDED BY THE LIGHT

Words and Music by
BRUCE SPRINGSTEEN

58

With a half-time feel

She got down,____ but she nev-er got tired. She's gon-na make it____ through__ the night.____ She's gon-na make it____ through____ the night.____

(Inst. solo ad lib....

# BRIDGE OVER TROUBLED WATER

Words and Music by
PAUL SIMON

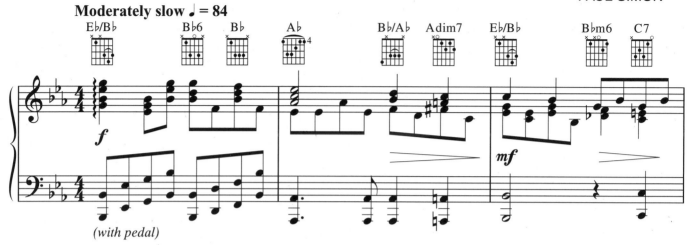

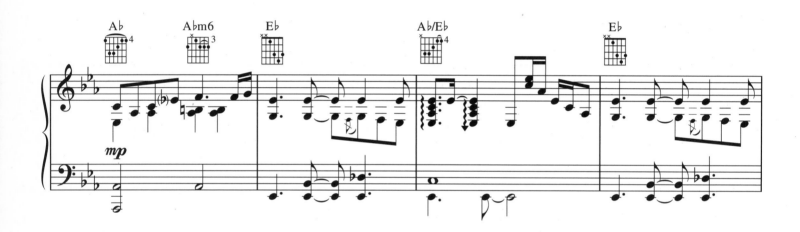

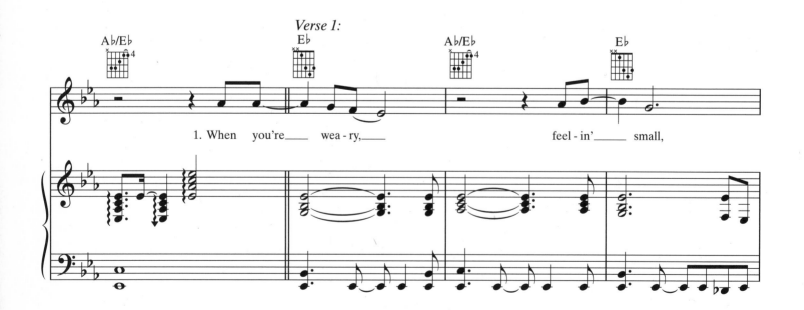

Verse 1:

1. When you're___ wea - ry,___ feel - in'___ small,

3. Sail on,____

____ sil - ver girl,____   sail on____ by.

*Verse 3:*

Bridge Over Troubled Water - 8 - 8

# BROWN SUGAR

Words and Music by
MICK JAGGER and KEITH RICHARDS

Brown Sugar - 7 - 1

76

78

*Guitar & Tenor Sax blues riff - Tenor Sax plays lower harmony (♭3)

Brown Sugar - 7 - 7

# CAT'S IN THE CRADLE

Words and Music by
HARRY CHAPIN and SANDY CHAPIN

80

silver spoon,_ Little Boy Blue and the man___ in the moon._

1.2. "When you com - in' home, Dad?" "I don't know when, but we'll get to - geth - er then,___
3. "When you com - in' home, Son?" "I don't know when, but we'll get to - geth - er then,___

___ Son. You know we'll have a good time then."
Dad. You know we'll have a good time

Cat's in the Cradle - 7 - 3

82

Cat's in the Cradle - 7 - 4

son's moved a - way. I called him up just the oth - er day.

I said, "I'd like to see___ you if you don't mind."_ He said, "I'd

love to, Dad,___ if I could find the time. You see, my

new job's a has - sle and the kids have the flu,___ but it's sure nice talk - in' to

you, Dad. It's been sure nice talk-in' to you."

And as I hung up the phone,__ it oc-curred to me,__ he'd

grown up just like me. My boy was just like

me.

*Chorus:*

And the cat's in the cra-dle and the

# (THEY LONG TO BE)
# CLOSE TO YOU

Words by
HAL DAVID

Music by
BURT BACHARACH

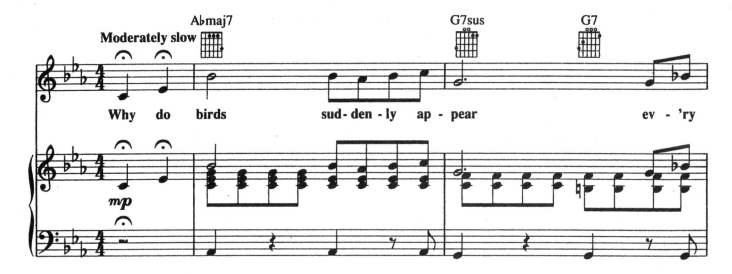

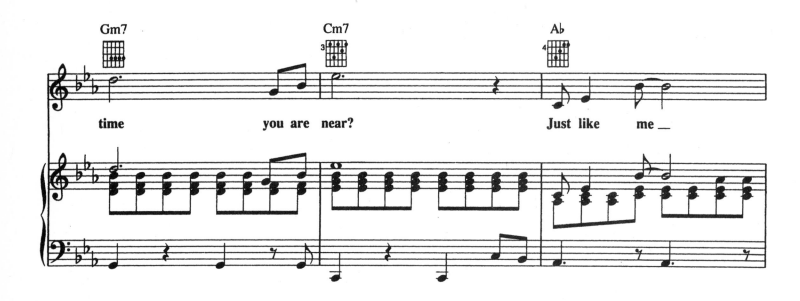

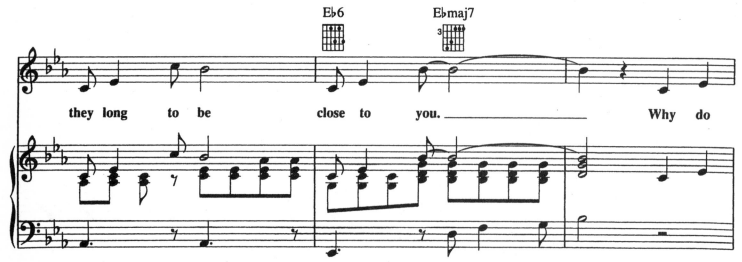

(They Long to Be) Close to You - 4 - 1

88
(They Long to Be) Close to You - 4 - 3

(They Long to Be) Close to You - 4 - 4

# DANCING QUEEN

Words and Music by
BENNY ANDERSSON, STIG ANDERSON
and BJORN ULVAEUS

Moderate disco beat ♩ = 104

*Chorus:*

# DON'T STOP 'TIL YOU GET ENOUGH

Written and Composed by
MICHAEL JACKSON

Don't Stop 'Til You Get Enough - 8 - 1

*Verse:*

1. Love - ly_____ is the feel - ing_____ now._____
2. Touch me_____ and I feel on_____ fire._____

Fe - ver,_____ tem-p'ra-tures
Ain't noth - ing_____ like a

ris - in'___ now._____ I'm
love de - sire._____

# DREAMS

Words and Music by
STEVIE NICKS

Dreams - 4 - 1

Dreams - 4 - 2

*Chorus:*

Fmaj7  G6  Fmaj7  G6

thun - der on - ly hap - pens when it's rain - ing.

Fmaj7  G6  Fmaj7  G6

Play-ers on - ly love___ you when they're play - ing.___ Say,

Fmaj7  G6  Fmaj7  G6

wom-en, they will come___ and they will go.___

Fmaj7  G6  Fmaj7  **1.** G6

When the rain___ wash - es___ you clean, you'll know.___ You'll

Dreams - 4 - 4

# DA YA THINK I'M SEXY?

Words and Music by
DUANE HITCHINGS, CARMINE APPICE
and ROD STEWART

Da Ya Think I'm Sexy? - 5 - 1

Da Ya Think I'm Sexy? - 5 - 2

# ESCAPE
## (The Piña Colada Song)

Words and Music by
RUPERT HOLMES

Escape - 5 - 1

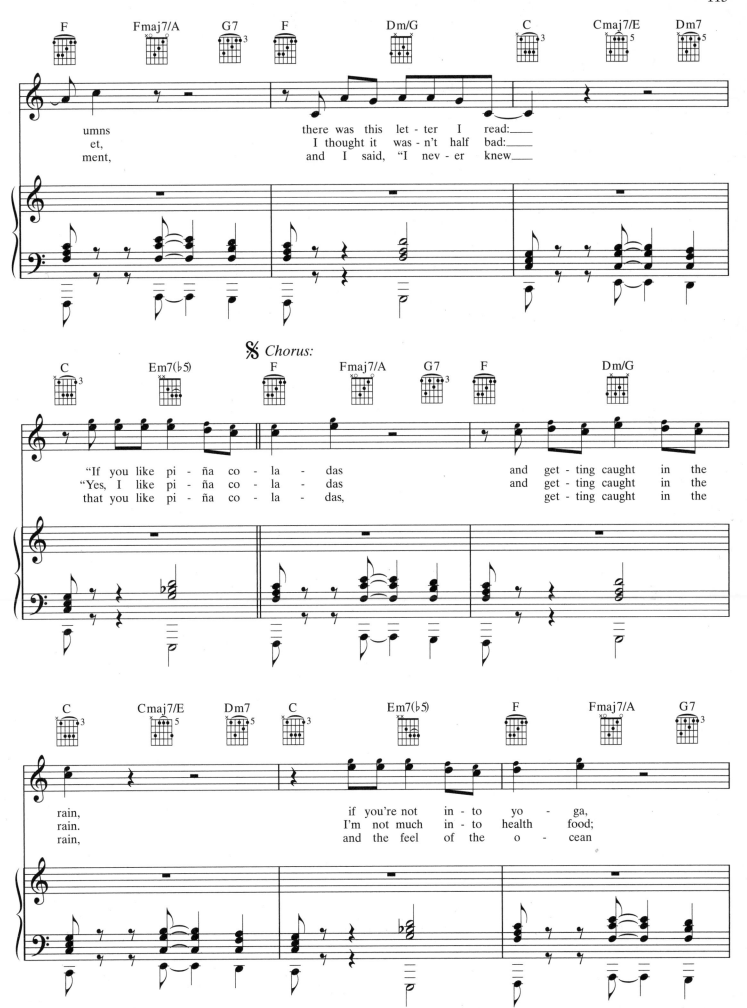

116

if you have half a brain,
I am in - to cham - pagne.
and the taste of cham - pagne.

if you like mak - ing love at
I've got to meet you by to -
If you'd like mak - ing love at

mid - night___
mor - row noon___
mid - night___

in the dunes on the Cape,
and cut through all this red tape,
in the dunes on the Cape,

then I'm the love that you've looked for.
at a bar called O' - Mal - ley's
you're the la - dy I've looked for.

Write to me and es -
where we'll plan our es -
Come with me and es -

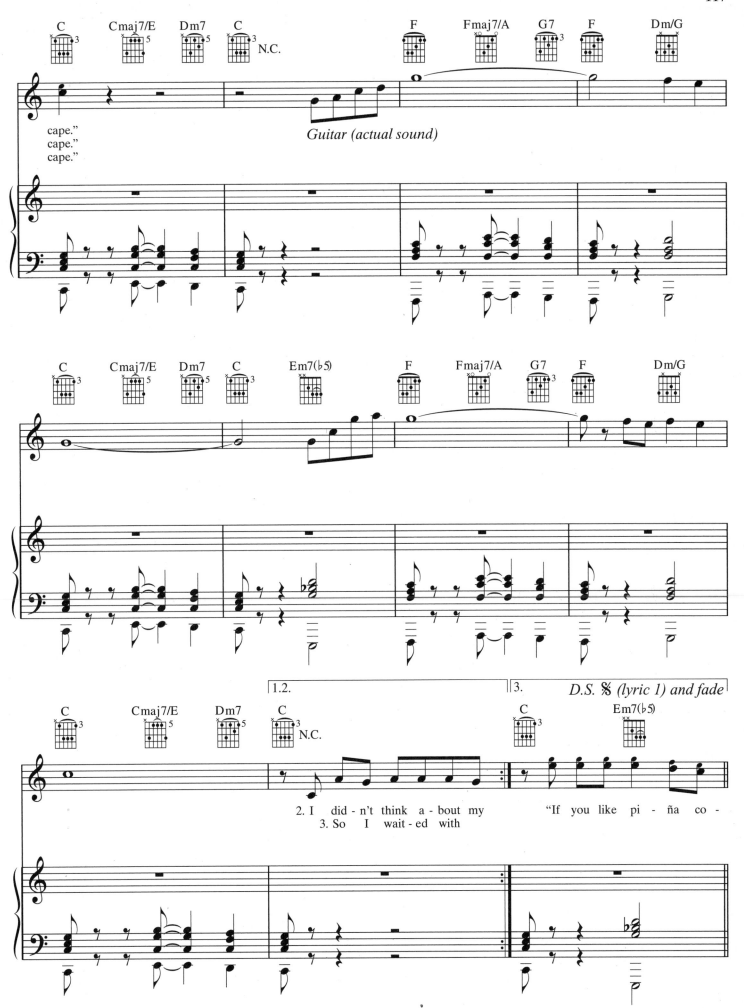

Guitar (actual sound)

cape."
cape."
cape."

2. I did - n't think a - bout my
3. So I wait - ed with

"If you like pi - ña co -

1.2.

3. D.S. 𝄋 (lyric 1) and fade

# EVERGREEN
### (Love Theme from *A Star Is Born*)

Words by
**PAUL WILLIAMS**

Music by
**BARBRA STREISAND**

**Moderately, with feeling**

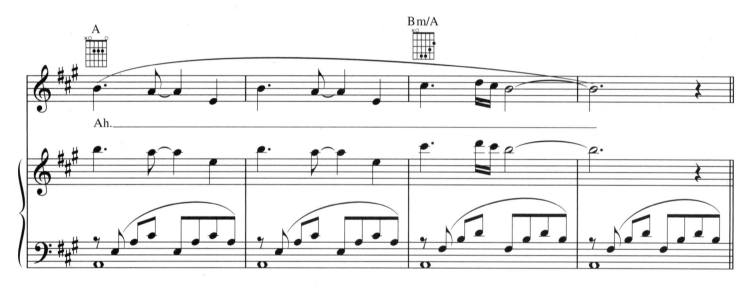

Ah.

Love,_____ soft as an eas-y chair;_____

Evergreen - 6 - 1

# GONNA FLY NOW

## (Theme from *Rocky*)

Words and Music by
BILL CONTI, AYN ROBBINS
and CAROL CONNORS

Feel-in' strong now._____

Won't be long now._____

Get-tin' strong now._____

128

# GREASE

**Moderately, with a beat**

Words and Music by
BARRY GIBB

*Verse 1:*

1. I solve my prob-lems and I see the light. We got a lov-in' thing.__ We got-ta feed it right.__

Grease - 5 - 1

fight right now.  We got to   be what we feel.  } Grease is  the word.
liev - ing now   that we can  be who we are.

It's got a groove,   it's got a mean - ing.

Grease is   the time,   is the place,   is the mo - tion.   Grease is   the way   we are feel-

*To Coda*

1.

ing.

2.

ing.

Grease - 5 - 3

# A HORSE WITH NO NAME

Words and Music by
DEWEY BUNNELL

136

A Horse with No Name - 5 - 3

138

A Horse with No Name - 5 - 5

# HOW DEEP IS YOUR LOVE

Words and Music by
BARRY GIBB, MAURICE GIBB
and ROBIN GIBB

1. I know your eyes in the morn - ing sun.___
2. I be - lieve in you.___
3. Na na na na na___

I feel you touch___ me in the pour - ing rain.___
You know the door___ to my ver - y soul.___
na na na na___ na na na na na.___

How Deep Is Your Love - 3 - 1

How Deep Is Your Love - 3 - 3

# HOT STUFF

Words and Music by
PETE BELLOTTE,
HAROLD FALTERMEIER,
and KEITH FORSEY

**Moderate disco** ♩ = 120

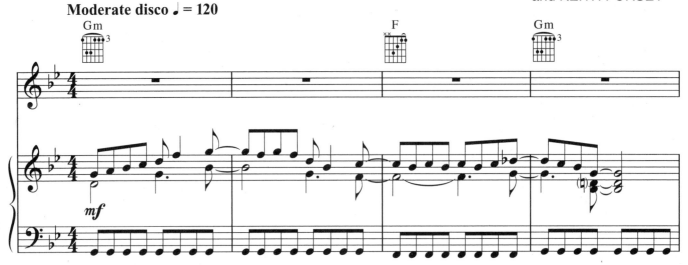

*Verse:*

1. Sit - tin' here___ eat - in' my heart___ out wait - in',
2. Look - in' for a lov - er who needs___ an - oth - er, don't

Hot Stuff - 6 - 1

Hot Stuff - 6 - 2

144

# HOTEL CALIFORNIA

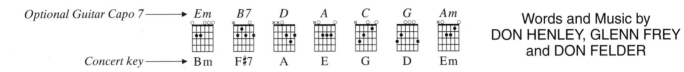

Words and Music by
DON HENLEY, GLENN FREY
and DON FELDER

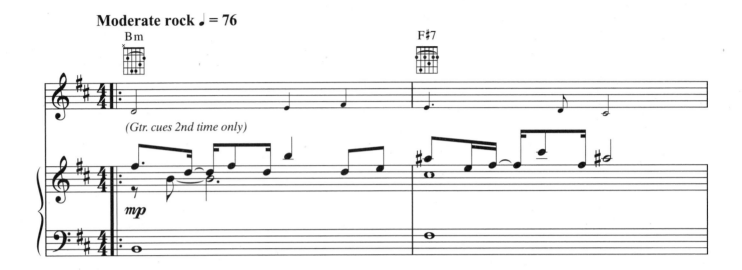

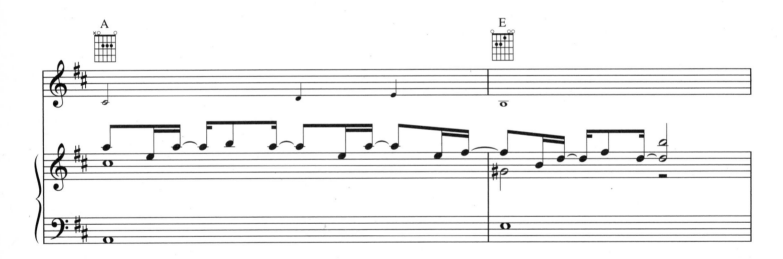

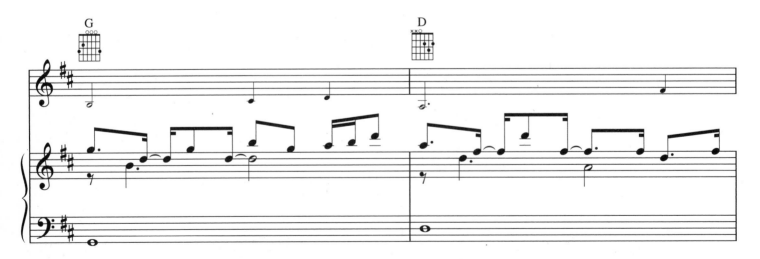

Hotel California - 8 - 1

*Verses 1 & 2:*

1. On a dark des-ert high-way, cool wind in my hair,
2. Her mind is Tif - fa - ny twist - ed, she got the Mer - ce - des bends.

warm_ smell of co-li - tas_ ris - ing up through the air._
She got a lot of pret-ty, pret-ty boys_ that she calls friends._

Up a - head in the dis - tance, I saw a shim-mer-ing light.
How they dance in the court - yard, sweet_ sum-mer sweat.

152

Hotel California - 8 - 5

# I CAN SEE CLEARLY NOW

Words and Music by
JOHNNY NASH

**Reggae** ♩ = 120

1. I can see clear - ly now,___ the rain___ is gone.___
2. Oh yes, I can make___ it now,___ the pain___ is gone.___
3. I can see clear - ly now,___ the rain___ is gone.___

I can see all___ ob - sta - cles___
All of the bad___ feel - ings have___
I can see all___ ob - sta - cles___

I Can See Clearly Now - 4 - 1

# I JUST WANT TO BE YOUR EVERYTHING

Words and Music by
BARRY GIBB

# I'LL BE THERE

Words and Music by
BERRY GORDY, HAL DAVIS,
WILLIE HUTCH and BOB WEST

**Moderately slow** ♩ = 92

*Verse 1:*

1. You and I must make a pact. We must bring sal-va-tion back.

Where there is love, I'll___ be there. (I'll be there.___)

*Verse 2:*

2. I'll reach out my hand to you. I'll have faith in all you do.___

I'll Be There - 4 - 1

*Verses 3 & 4:*

3. Let me fill your heart with joy and laugh-ter. To-geth-er-ness, well, that's
4. If you should ev-er find some-one new, I know he'd bet-ter be

all I'm af-ter.
good to you,

When-ev-er you need me,
'cause if he does-n't,

I'll

*To Coda*

be there. (I'll be there.) I'll be there to pro-tect

you with an un-self-ish love that re-spects you.

# KILLING ME SOFTLY WITH HIS SONG

Words and Music by
CHARLES FOX and NORMAN GIMBEL

Strum-ming my pain with his fin - gers, sing-ing my life with his words.

Kill - ing me soft - ly with his song, kill - ing me soft -

ly with his song, tell - ing my whole life with his

172

Ab    Db    Bbm7

I____ heard he had a style.___    And so I came_
em - bar - rassed by the crowd.___    I felt he found_
in____ all my dark de - spair.___    And then he looked_

Eb7    Fm

____ to see___ him, to lis - ten for___ a while.___
____ my let - ters and read each one___ out loud.___
____ right through___ me, as if I was - n't there.___

Bbm7    Eb7    Ab

And there___ he was,___ this young boy,    a strang - er to_
I prayed_ that he___ would fin - ish,    but he just kept_
And he___ just kept___ on sing - ing,    sing - ing clear_

%  *Chorus:*

C7    Fm    Bbm7

____ my eyes...___ }    Strum - ming my pain___ with his fin - gers,___
____ right on...___ }
____ and strong...___ }

Killing Me Softly With His Song - 6 - 3

174

# LE FREAK

Words and Music by
BERNARD EDWARDS and NILE RODGERS

Le Freak - 3 - 1

Big fun— to be had by ev-'ry-one.— It's up to you.— It
Feel the rhy-thm. Chant the rhyme.. Come on a-long— and

sure-ly can be done.— Young and old are
have a real good time.— Like the days of

do-in' it,— I'm told. Just one try and
stomp-in' at the Sa-voy, now we Freak.

you, too, will be sold.— It's called "Le Freak." They're
Oh, what a joy.— Just come on down

# LEAN ON ME

Words and Music by
BILL WITHERS

**Medium Gospel Ballad**

Lean on Me - 7 - 1

184

Lean on Me - 7 - 6

185

Lean on Me - 7 - 7

# MAGGIE MAY

**Words and Music by
ROD STEWART and MARTIN QUITTENTON**

Moderately fast ♩ = 132

1. Wake up, Mag-gie, I think I got some-thin' to say to you.___ It's
2. 3. 4. *See additional lyrics*

late Sep-tem-ber and I real-ly should_ be back___ at__ school. I

Maggie May - 4 - 1

Repeat ad lib. and fade

2. I'll

*Verse 2:*
The morning sun, when it's in your face, really shows your age.
But that don't worry me none; in my eyes you're ev'rything.
I laughed at all of your jokes; my love you didn't need to coax.
Oh, Maggie, I couldn't have tried any more.
You led me away home, just to save you from being alone.
You stole my soul, and that's a pain I can do without.

*Verse 3:*
All I needed was a friend to lend a guiding hand.
But you turned into a lover, and, Mother, what a lover! You wore me out.
All you did was wreck my bed, and in the morning kick me in the head.
Oh, Maggie, I couldn't have tried any more.
You led me away home, 'cause you didn't want to be alone.
You stole my heart; I couldn't leave you if I tried.

*Verse 4:*
I suppose I could collect my books and get on back to school,
Or steal my Daddy's cue and make a living out of playin' pool,
Or find myself a rock 'n' roll band that needs a helpin' hand.
Oh, Maggie, I wish I'd never seen your face.
You made a first-class fool out of me, but I'm as blind as a fool can be.
You stole my heart, but I love you anyway.

# MAMA TOLD ME (NOT TO COME)

Words and Music by
RANDY NEWMAN

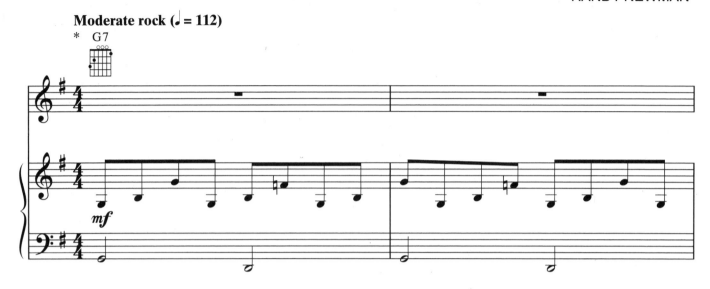

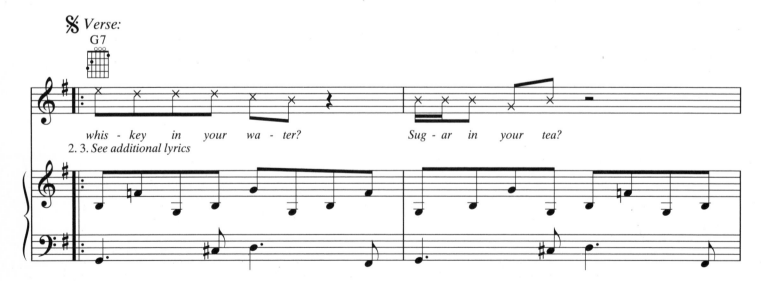

* Original recording in A♭ Major

Mama Told Me (Not to Come) - 6 - 2

192

194

Verse 2:
(Spoken:)
*Open up the window, let some air into this room.*
*I think I'm almost chokin' from the smell of stale perfume.*
*And that cigarette you're smokin' 'bout scare me half to death.*
*Open up the window, sucker, let me catch my breath.*
(To Chorus:)

Verse 3:
(Spoken:)
*The radio is blastin', someone's knockin' at the door.*
*I'm lookin' at my girlfriend; she's passed out on the floor.*
*I seen so many things I ain't never seen before.*
*Don't know what it is; I don't wanna see no more.*
(To Chorus:)

# ME AND MRS. JONES

Words and Music by
KENNETH GAMBLE, LEON HUFF
and CARY GILBERT

to let it go now.____

We got-ta be ex-tra care-ful____

that we don't build our hopes up too high,____

'cause she's____ got her own ob-li-ga-tions,____

202

# THE MOST BEAUTIFUL GIRL

Words and Music by
NORRIS WILSON, BILLY SHERRILL
and RORY BOURKE

Moderately ♩ = 108

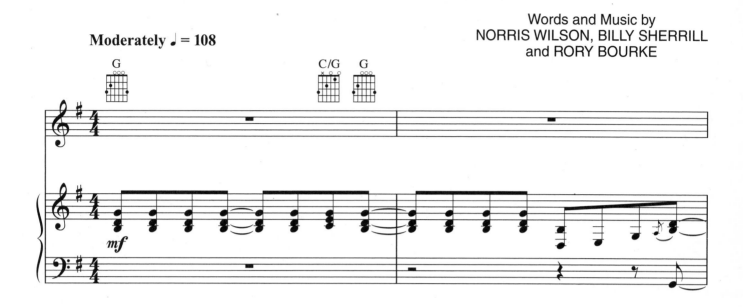

%  *Chorus:*

{Hey,___} {hey,___} did you hap-pen to see___ the most beau-ti-ful girl___ in the world?___

The Most Beautiful Girl - 5 - 1

# MY SHARONA

Words and Music by
DOUG FEIGER and BERTON AVERRE

# YOU NEEDED ME

Words and Music by
RANDY GOODRUM

**Very slowly and smoothly (♩ = 63)**

I cried a tear, you wiped it dry. I was con-

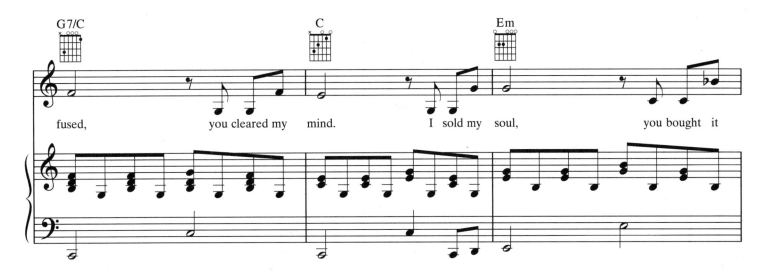

fused, you cleared my mind. I sold my soul, you bought it

You Needed Me - 5 - 1

217

You Needed Me - 5 - 5

# ONE OF THESE NIGHTS

Words and Music by
DON HENLEY and GLENN FREY

One of these nights,
one of these crazy old nights
we're gon-na find out, pret-ty ma-ma, what turns on your lights.

dreams,
one of these lost and lone-ly dreams;
we're gon-na find one, one that real-ly screams.

One of These Nights - 4 - 1

# PLAY THAT FUNKY MUSIC

Words and Music by
ROBERT PARISSI

**Moderate funk** ♩ = 108

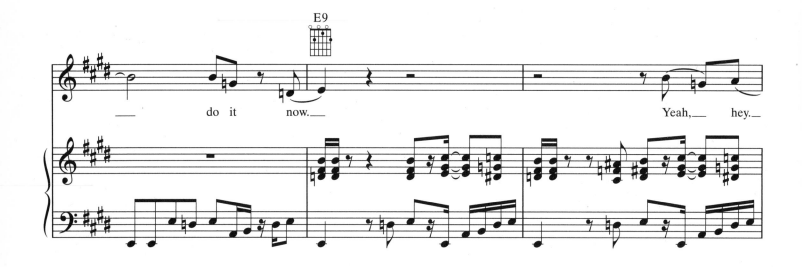

playin' in a rock and roll band.___
changin' rock and roll in' minds.___

I nev-er had no prob-lems,___
And things were get-tin' shak-y.___

___ yeah,

burn-in' down the one-night stands.___
I thought I'd have to leave it be -

___ hind.

And
But

ev-'ry-thing a-round me,___
now it's so much bet-ter.___

224

Chorus:

226

play that funk - y mu - sic till you die,     till you die,_____

—     oh,_____ till you die."_____     Come on,

play some e - lec - tri - fied funk - y mu - sic.     (Inst. solo ad lib....

# RICH GIRL

Words and Music by
DARYL HALL

Rich Girl - 4 - 1

You can re-ly___ on the old man's mon-ey, you can re-ly___ on the old man's mon-ey. It's a

bitch girl, but it's gone too far 'cause you know it does-n't mat-ter an-y-way.___

Say, mon - ey, mon-ey won't get you too far, Say, mon - ey, mon-ey won't get you too far,

Say, mon - ey, mon-ey won't get you too far, get you too far.___ And you say___

**Repeat and Fade**

you can re-ly___ on the old man's mon-ey, you can re-ly___ on the old man's mon-ey. You're a

# SISTER GOLDEN HAIR

Words and Music by
GERRY BECKLEY

Well, I tried ___

Sister Golden Hair - 4 - 1

Sister Golden Hair - 4 - 4

# SOUTHERN NIGHTS

Words and Music by
ALLEN TOUSSAINT

Southern Nights - 4 - 1

# STAYIN' ALIVE

Words and Music by
BARRY GIBB, MAURICE GIBB
and ROBIN GIBB

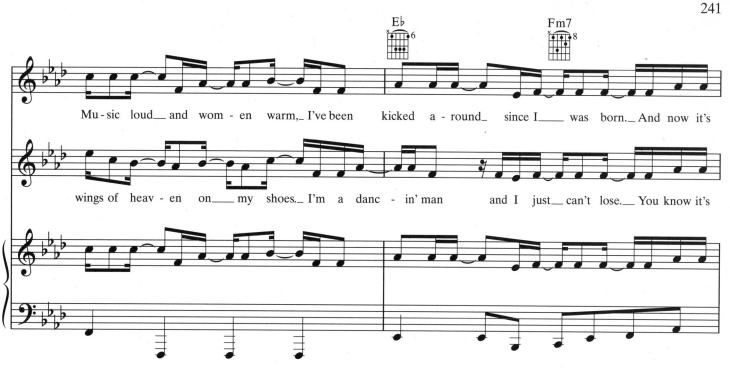

Mu - sic loud__ and wom - en warm,_ I've been kicked a - round_ since I__ was born. And now it's
wings of heav - en on__ my shoes._ I'm a danc - in' man and I just__ can't lose. You know it's

(1. 2. 3.) all right,__ it's o - kay,__ and you may look__ the oth - er way,__ but

we can try__ to un - der - stand__ the New York Times'_ ef - fect__ on man.__

# SUNDOWN

Words and Music by
GORDON LIGHTFOOT

\* **Guitarists:** Please note that the chord diagrams are in the key of E but the piano accompaniment is in the key of F.
In order for the guitar to sound in the same key as the piano, use a capo on the 1st fret.
You also may adjust the capo to play in any key that fits your own individual vocal range.

Sundown - 4 - 1

Coda

my back stairs._ Sun - down, you bet - ter take care_ if I

find you bin creep-in' round_ my back stairs.._ Some-times I

think it's a sin _ when I feel like I'm win-nin' when I'm los-in' a - gain. _

# SUNSHINE ON MY SHOULDERS

Words by
JOHN DENVER

Music by
JOHN DENVER, MIKE TAYLOR
and DICK KNISS

# SUPERSTITION

Moderate funk ♩ = 104

Words and Music by
STEVIE WONDER

Superstition - 6 - 1

Su - per - sti - tion ain't the way._____

*(Horns)*

*Repeat ad lib. and fade*

# THANK YOU
## (Falettinme Be Mice Elf Agin)

Words and Music by
SYLVESTER STEWART

**Moderate funk** ♩ = 108

*(Horns, 2nd time only)*

*Verses 1, 2, & 3:*

1. Look - in' at the dev - il,
2. Stiff all in the col - lar;
3. Dance___ to the mu - sic

Thank You (Falettinme Be Mice Elf Agin) - 6 - 1

262

Chorus:

Thank You (Falettinme Be Mice Elf Agin) - 6 - 3

264

*Verse 4:*

Chorus:

# TIME IN A BOTTLE

Words and Music by
JIM CROCE

Time in a Bottle - 4 - 1

268

# TOO MUCH HEAVEN

Words and Music by
BARRY GIBB, MAURICE GIBB
and ROBIN GIBB

# UNDERCOVER ANGEL

Words and Music by
ALAN O'DAY

Moderate funk groove ♩ = 96

1. Cry - in' on__ my pil - low,_____ lone - ly in__ my bed;_____
2. 3. *See additional lyrics*

then I heard a voice__ be - side__ me and she soft - ly said,

Undercover Angel - 6 - 1

*Chorus:*

280

*Verse 2:*
Heavenly surrender, sweet afterglow,
Givin' up my heart to you,
Now, angel, don't go.
She said, "Go find the right one,
Love her and then
When you look into her eyes
You'll see me again."
I said, "What?"
She said, "Ooo-wee."
I said, "All right!"
She said, "Love me, love me, love me."
*(To Chorus:)*

*Verse 3:*
Now you know my story,
And, girl, if it's right,
I'm gonna take you in my arms
And love you tonight.
Underneath the covers
The answer lies.
I'm lookin' for my angel
In your sweet lovin' eyes.
She said, "What?"
I said, "Ooo-wee."
She said, "All right!"
I said, "Get next to me."
She said, "What?"
I said, "Ooo-wee."
She said, "All right!"
I said, "Love me, love me, love me."
*(To Chorus:)*

# WHAT A FOOL BELIEVES

Words and Music by
KENNY LOGGINS and MICHAEL McDONALD

284

# YOU DON'T BRING ME FLOWERS

Words by
NEIL DIAMOND, MARILYN BERGMAN
and ALAN BERGMAN

Music by
NEIL DIAMOND

You Don't Bring Me Flowers - 4 - 1

# YOU'RE THE ONE THAT I WANT

Words and Music by
JOHN FARRAR

You're the One that I Want - 4 - 1

294

You're the One that I Want - 4 - 3

# YOU'VE GOT A FRIEND

Words and Music by
CAROLE KING

298

# YOU LIGHT UP MY LIFE

Words and Music by
JOE BROOKS

You Light Up My Life - 3 - 1